TABLE OF CONTENT

INTRODUCTION

A nonprofit organization is an institution that is an emanation of civil society. It sits right between corporations (which are driven by profit) and the government (which is ideally not driven by profit but rather by public and national interests). Nonprofit organizations are a recent invention. We can trace their existence to the foundation of the Red Cross by Henry Dunant, who decided to intervene on the battlefield of Solferino (Italy) after the French and Austrian armies met, leaving thousands of soldiers agonizing. The Swiss social activist saw by himself that the absence of incentives from both sides to take into consideration humanitarian needs called for the kind of initiative that would be at the origin of the Red Cross. It does not mean however that social and political initiatives that were not

motivated by profit did not exist before Henry Dunant. The Catholic Church, for example, has a well-documented, albeit criticized, history of organizing relief operations and humanitarian initiatives to cater to the poor, the sick and the disabled. However, these organizations were all affiliated to a central institution, the Church, which had incentives to act in such a way as it was a source of political capital in pre-secular Europe. Nonprofit organizations on the other hand act out from the genuine desire to address social and humanitarian issues, with no ambition to translate their actions into economic and political terms. While they can be affiliated to an institution, nonprofits are usually created by a group of individuals who do not belong to a chain of command or a hierarchy; nonprofits are therefore somewhat independent from the pressures traditionally associated with collective, social impact work.

Nowadays, nonprofit organizations are more important than ever as they allow individual citizens to contribute to change. Corporations have no incentive to act beyond the perspective of profit; we cannot expect, from a systemic point of view, that for-profit organizations can step up and tackle social issues. Milton Friedman argues that for-profit organizations have only one social responsibility: generate profits in the most efficient and optimized way for their shareholders. In the study of corporate social responsibility, this approach is known as the minimalist approach. Other theories support that corporations have a social responsibility that goes beyond the profit imperative: they both benefit and impact collectivities and communities; they are therefore bounded to some contractual obligations towards them.

The government on the other hand is often limited by financial means, political bias and ideology. In democratic, representative states, the appeal to public approval is also a limiting factor when it comes to government action. The rationale for nonprofit organizations stems therefore from this duality which leaves unaddressed some of the issues that plague humanity, because no actor has the incentives nor the means to tackle them.

In this book, we will explore the intricacies of setting up your own nonprofit organization. We will discuss the drivers behind such a choice and present 7 concrete steps to succeed. After reading this, you will truly understand how the nonprofit model works and be ready to create one yourself successfully!

STEP 1

UNDERSTANDING THE NONPROFIT MODEL

HOW DOES NONPROFIT WORK?
To be able to succeed in the nonprofit world, you must secure an understanding of how a nonprofit works and how it interacts with others.

A nonprofit organization is characterized by the fact that its brand recognition is centered around accountability, openness, transparency and honesty. It has a different accountability structure as it is mainly accountable to volunteers, founders, members, employees and donors. Such a structure entails a different managerial approach

which we will detail in the dedicated section. A nonprofit organization must formulate stable goals, methods and funding. It must sustain continuous activity and ensure members are selected after a rigorous process that ensures candidates have the necessary skills to contribute and have the same values, drive, motivation and mindset the organization is promoting. There are no legal obligations to donate to a nonprofit; volunteers are not engaged in binding contracts, as membership and financial contributions cannot be mandatory. Employees, on the other hand, do have stated contractual obligations in the context of the labor law.

Nonprofit organizations start by defining their ultimate mission, which consists in the pursuit of a public purpose. It can take the form of fighting poverty, disease or violence. It can also focus on promoting ideas and ideals; religious, educational and militant nonprofit organizations do formulate a world vision their actions are supposed to fulfill. A not-for-profit organization can operate on many levels. The local level by organizing communities, tabling on grassroots movements and tendencies and capitalizing on local people's organizations. It can act on the national level, country-wide, interacting with authorities and other social stakeholders. It can operate on the international level, taking responsibility for promoting its ideals and fulfilling its mission beyond its native land. Finally, it can have global engagement by integrating with international organizations that help and structure their actions. Every level of activity implies a different approach to management.

Beyond purely humanitarian causes, many civil society movements find their roots in the late 19th and 20th in ideological and social movements like the women's rights movement, the anti-apartheid and anti-segregation movement or the anti-globalization organizations. They have also been shaped by the political clashes between interest groups advocating for legislative changes (pro-gun movements, gay rights, pro-choice vs. pro-life etc.). As a consequence, it is often necessary for a nonprofit organization that wants to have an impact on the social contract to take a stance. For example, the American Civil Liberties Union, in its quest for justice, has supported civil rights movements and sued states and legislatures that advanced voters' suppression measures and laws. As a consequence, it has often found itself on the political left in the United States, often confronting right-wing politicians and initiatives.

Nonprofit does not mean that the organization does not make money; it often does, as it needs resources to be somewhat financially independent and have stable cashflows to plan on the long term. Indeed, donations are not predictable as they depend on a wide range of factors. Government sponsorship is subject to political changes and corporate sponsorships can compromise a nonprofit's brand by associating it to eventual corporate malpractices. Nonprofit organizations are designated by this term because of the non-distribution clause. Founders, executives and managers cannot derive personal financial gains from the money the nonprofit organization makes. They are not shareholders who are entitled to receive dividends, as it is admitted that these actors got into the nonprofit business to promote a cause, not make money. From an organizational perspective, the main difference between for profit and nonprofit is the fact that the latter channel their earnings into the organization's activities, to continue pursuing their mission.

The activities of nonprofit organizations are diverse. Some organizations work primarily as advocacy groups, which consists of targeting decision-makers and public opinion to raise awareness about specific issues. It does not produce or distribute goods or services (if it does it is as a way to raise funds, not in the context of its core activity). They represent the needs and rights of individuals or specific groups (political prisoners, refugees etc.).

Others work by directly providing goods and services that satisfy the physical requirements of some individuals or groups. It generally consists of giving free meals, clothes or medical assistance to those who cannot afford them. Their activities are seen as complementary work to some deficiencies the government, the market and society in general struggle to tackle.

PROS AND CONS OF THE NONPROFIT STATUS
The nonprofit model is very interesting; it is a powerful tool that allows you to take control and have a real, tangible impact where you won't change.

The nonprofit format has advantages, both for society and for individual stakeholders themselves. First, it allows citizens to take the initiative and promote impactful actions and ideas that are not addressed by the government or by for-profit organizations. Second, the nonprofit imperative means that all the resources are dedicated to the pursuit of the mission. It is also a guarantee that every individual involved has no motive to enrich himself, reinforcing the idea that members, founders and volunteers are acting out of intrinsic motivation for the cause they are promoting. Third, this type of organization is not subject to taxation, meaning that all the resources it can gather are fully invested in the organization's activity. The rationale behind it is that since this type of structure is complementary to the government's mission, it cannot be taken into consideration for fiscal purposes as it does not aim to

produce economic value, but social welfare. Fourth, in the majority of countries, there exists a legal framework that ensures nonprofit organizations stay dedicated to the cause they are promoting. Such legal context guarantees to stakeholders (donors, volunteers and members) that the government regulates the activity of such organizations and that they remain solely driven by the mission they have chosen to accomplish. Finally, there is a great advantage of being a nonprofit organization in terms of public relations. It allows a collection of citizens to take a public stance without being picked apart by critics. The only scenario where nonprofit organizations are criticized is when they behave wrongly and fail to pursue the goals it has mobilized resources to accomplish. Therefore, nonprofit organizations have public relations' capital that reduces the friction between them and the two other types of organizations.

However, there are some limitations and frustrations that come with creating and running a nonprofit organization. Some are directly linked to the nature of nonprofit organizations, others to the modalities they operate in. For example, this kind of organization does not have access to the direct levers of power, in order to influence the status quo. It must rely on indirect forms, like lobbying or public campaigning to change public opinion, which in turn pressures decision-makers. Nonprofit organizations are often constrained financially as they rely on outside funding, which constitutes the majority of their financing. They must strike a balance between integrity and financial relevance. This imperative had nonprofit organizations in the 1990s get closer to corporations, selling them the idea that they could advise for-profit firms to behave in a more responsible way and that the association with a known nonprofit would help them foster a positive image. However, with the series of corporate malpractices that followed that period, it appeared evident that corporations were incentivized to have a minimalist approach to corporate social responsibility and the association to misbehaving corporations became a public relations problem for nonprofits. Today we live an era where nonprofits are actively criticizing corporate functioning and building financial autonomy from them. It is partly due to the development of Internet that has made donations easier and cheaper. Moreover, the rise of social networks provided nonprofits with powerful campaigning tools.

FUTURE PERSPECTIVES
Since nonprofit organizations are primarily businesses that generate and manage resources to fund a specific endeavor rather than enrich stockholders, it is facing more or less the same shifts and disruptions the entire economic sector faces in the 2020s. Indeed, nonprofits are increasingly confronted with the necessity of optimizing processes and capturing new "market shares" as the offer increases and diversifies. What are the future challenges and opportunities nonprofits will face in the next decade and what winning at the nonprofit game will imply in terms of changes?

The most notable shift is undoubtedly the generalization of technology and the shifts in its cost structure. The changes it has brought to the entire activity span from communication to internal management and information management. Computation power has witnessed decreasing costs and increasing returns, and in a world where data is the primary commodity for businesses and organizations, it has forced them to invest massively in information technology and data analysis to predict, detect patterns of behavior and have a precise knowledge of their target audience. Technology has also changed the way entities communicate and spread their message, which has made customer engagement much more complicated as it depends now on a variety of variables and requires a massive input of data. Businesses face the challenge of adapting their brand and communication channels to the predominance of social media and the centrality of genuine customer engagement, with a vision that is more focused on customer value rather than the product itself. These changes come as challenges to entities that face them, but they also constitute great opportunities as they will prompt them to work on transparency, accountability and trustworthiness, all of which are decisive for nonprofits.

Such shifts are especially important for nonprofits as they face a changing market, with new generations (millennials and generation Z) which are much more involved in social activism and willing to contribute to solving public issues. The "market" for nonprofits tackling vital issues has grown exponentially and so has their ability to reach, pitch, convince and create social links. New technology has to be leveraged to meet the challenges of catering to millions of individuals who have both the awareness to support them and the inner motivation to have an active role personally. Nonprofits will have to rethink membership and donations, with the introduction of e-volunteering and the ease of use for fintech, e-commerce and other digital innovations. They will also have to adapt their marketing and communication to younger people, meaning that understanding new public relations trends and channels will provide an edge.

Furthermore, the range of issues that are now attracting public attention is growing. Nonprofits can choose to tackle a number of new public concerns like mental health or digital rights which will find an echo in the population. These new issues will involve a redesign of the nonprofit models of governance and ways of doing business.

All these changes cannot be tackled by individual organizations, which implies that collaboration with other nonprofits and other types of actors will be decisive. Nonprofits must develop models that rely on cooperation and foster a collaborative culture and mindset. Both technology and market changes will open doors for more effective partnering. Nonprofits will have to mobilize resources and open channels of collaboration to benefit from these novelties.

STEP 2

LEGAL CONSIDERATIONS FOR SETTING A NONPROFIT ORGANIZATION

GENERAL INFORMATION

The nonprofit status is not self-evident and certainly not always an adapted structure to tackle the whole range of issues. It is therefore vital to invest the time, energy and resources to correctly undergo due diligence and determine whether this model is the most adapted to what you are aiming for.

The initial steps are first to document all the aspects of the issue you are willing to work on. Depending on the nature of the issue, technical research might be necessary (if you are targeting health issues for example). However all nonprofits must have a clear, well-documented idea about the business model and its viability over time. You have to consider if the nonprofit model is indeed the most adapted to the business environment since not all public issues can be tackled in a nonprofit way.

For example, fighting pollution and global warming has prompted the emergence of a wide range of for-profit businesses that place profitability at the center of their business model since they are relying on massive capital investment for research & development and asset investment. Companies that manufacture CO_2-recycling stations that suck the gas out of the atmosphere to turn it into green fuel or contain it underground had to adopt a for-profit structure, as they were relying on both the investments from oil companies and their ability to integrate the recycled fuel in the distribution network.

It is also essential to make sure you have the ability to mobilize the right people for managing your organization. You cannot consider starting a nonprofit by yourself or leaving recruitment to chance. When it comes to attracting employees and talent, nonprofits have a disadvantage compared to the private or public sectors, as they are limited by law in terms of overhead administrative costs. Nonprofits cannot therefore compete with other organizations in terms of compensation; it has to rely on self-motivated employees to derive value from their responsibilities rather than from their pay. This is why you have to make sure you can immediately access like-minded individuals who can help you startup your nonprofit out of genuine interest and engagement for your cause. We will further detail the managerial challenges of nonprofits in chapter 5.

You must also be able to see the big picture in which your organization will have to fit. You must consider the risks your business model exposes your organization to and they can be mitigated. You will also have to consider your place on the market, as you do not want to be a duplicate of existing nonprofits; implying that you have to think in advance of the unique voice or ways you can bring to the table. When drafting your purpose statements, do not pinpoint any precise issue that could lose its relevance over time. Define a broad problem and the different steps that could lead to its mitigation overtime, with an emphasis on how your organization aims at contributing to the solution.

Finally, you need to define the legal boundaries that limit your action if you choose the nonprofit status. So many elements could cause you to lose your tax-exempt status, like lobbying, political activism or violating specific regulations. As a nonprofit you will be exposed to risks that range from labor law compliance to conflicts of interests and limits on your ability to communicate, advocate or act.

SETTING UP A NONPROFIT IN THE UNITED STATES: LEGAL FRAMEWORK
In the United States, nonprofits generally work under the 501(c) organization status. A 501(c) organization is a nonprofit organization that is structured according to Section 501(c) of the U.S Federal Code. The 501(c) is one of 29 types of nonprofit organizations that can qualify for federal tax exemptions. These organizations have no defined limits in the funds they can receive from donations, contributions, grants and sponsorships, which makes it advantageous but also imposes scrutiny from the Internal Revenue Service (IRS)

Under section 501(c), a nonprofit can apply for tax-exemption it works primarily to promote a cause that is charitable, religious, educational, scientific or literary. Sports associations are also included, as well as those who advocate against a child or animal abuse.

TAXATION, EXEMPTION AND THE IRS

A nonprofit organization starts at the state level, when founders fill in the legal requirements and establish headquarters. After this initial stage, the organization can obtain recognition of tax-exempt status by applying for it at federal level and filling the IRS paperwork. The IRS reviews the application to make sure the organization indeed contributes to an eligible nonprofit cause and issues the tax-exempt organization status. Governance guidelines must be respected in order to be recognized by the IRS. The overhead administrative costs must be kept in line with regulation to avoid that wages are used to channel the nonprofit's resources to employees and founders. Other criteria for the governance of nonprofits are also evaluated.

The tax exemption is crucial as it allows for tax-deductible donations, therefore inciting potential donors to make a contribution and reduce their income tax expense. Moreover, the organization itself sees its taxation brought to a minimum, with the exception of secondary federal taxes like employment taxes. A nonprofit will not have to pay "income" tax like a for-profit organization but will have to pay charges for its employees in the context of labor law and state guidelines. A tax-exempt organization will, however, pay federal tax on income that is derived from non-core activities (like investment revenues).

The exemptions that apply to nonprofits include property tax, sales tax and VAT. One must differentiate between the federal tax system and the local/state tax

system, as an exemption at the federal level does not guarantee an exception at the local level. Such an advantageous tax position does not exempt an organization from rigorously filing its tax documents; the IRS will consider any lack of disclosure according to guidelines to be fraudulent, which can lead to losing the tax-exempt status. Such filings allow both the IRS and the public to make sure the organization is operating legitimately, and nonprofits that aim at promoting trustworthiness, transparency and accountability have every incentive to report their financial position.

SETTING UP A NONPROFIT IN EUROPE

In the United Kingdom it is possible to choose from a wide variety of statutes. One can choose to simply organize an unincorporated structure that does not have any legal recognition apart from a declaration of purpose. Most groups that cater to local issues in communities and have a grassroots nature tend to prefer this approach, as their core activities do not need the infrastructure the other statutes provide.

When considering more complex structures, you have to take into account the way your nonprofit will generate income and raise funds. Charitable organizations that rely purely on donations and grants and do not have overhead administrative costs usually go for the various charity models the UK legislation provides. Volunteers are considered to be the main stakeholders in such organizations and conflicts of interests are virtually nonexistent.

Organizations that plan on deriving income from the sale of goods and services are called social enterprises. This denomination implies that the proceeds from such activities will be purely dedicated to funding the nonprofit's initiatives. However it is not a legal status per se, as these organizations incorporate according to different variants. Organizations that place voting members at the center of its decision-making process are also subject to different regulations.

All statutes impose strict bookkeeping and transparency conditions that are thoroughly audited by the competent

authorities. Books must be kept and updated regularly to document the sources and uses of funds. Compliance with labor law is also controlled and overhead administrative costs must be justified and maintained under a specific ratio.

STEP 3

HOW TO SECURE FUNDING?

THE BASICS OF FUNDRAISING

To be successful as a nonprofit, you must be able to master the art of fundraising and develop a unique approach to your communication. It is vitally important that you understand why it is so important for the current and future existence of your organization, how it works and the mistakes you need to avoid.

Fundraising is one of the main sources of income for a nonprofit. It has strategic importance as it allows an organization to generate stable, predictable cash flows that fund its activities and give it the means to plan its course of action. Stability is a key element because it provides you with a time horizon over which you can formulate a strategy and articulate your communication.

The most common mistakes which put a strain on a starting nonprofit usually come from not having the proper mindset. Organizations often consider donors as customers in the narrowest sense, which is a key misconception. You are not selling them anything, you are trying to communicate around the value of what you do (or trying to do); how investing in your organization can help tackle an issue or raise awareness. It is about building credibility and brand recognition by demonstrating that you are determined to work to make the world a better place and that it aligns with their principles and values. Donors are, therefore not customers, they are partners. You are building a relationship based on trust and shared values and principles, and every action you undertake must take into account the impact on the drivers of donors' acquisition.

Furthermore, you should not be harassing donors for

their money, especially regular donors. It gives them the impression you are begging for their attention and money and can be seen as a red flag. If the majority of your emails and newsletters revolves around donations, you might be perceived as either too greedy, dishonest or utterly incompetent.

Finally, a successful nonprofit understands that donations are not free money. Indeed, fundraising has a cost structure that varies according to the forms it takes. Even setting a website and online payment infrastructure costs money; it is a fixed cost that needs to be taken into account when evaluating net donations. Therefore, you must map out your cost structure and aim at optimizing it to reduce the overhead administrative and technical costs to maximize your profits.

HOW TO FUNDRAISE EFFICIENTLY?
To be able to fundraise effectively, you will first have deploy a narrative, a vision, for the current fundraising cycle (usually a year). In order to do that, you will have to pitch a specific, realistic objective that you can accomplish in that timeframe. For example, you cannot organize a fundraising campaign and ask for donations to "fight global warming." But you can collect donations to help mitigate the effects of rising sea levels in a specific area by deploying resources and funds to help build infrastructure for local fishing villages in the Mekong Delta. Formulating a precise and specific objective that is both attainable and relevant to your cause is the way to go!

Second, you have to draw realistic expectations from your fundraising initiatives. When planning and programming your budget for the year, do not set absurd benchmarks based on unrealistic assumptions ("we can pitch this idea to Bill Gates, he will certainly help us"). Think about realistic projections, your goal must be based on a realistic assessment of your growth trend. You cannot expect your fundraising to go from $200,000 to a million in just a year! It is consistency rather than one-hits you are looking for, because not only will it fit right in your organic growth but will also help you plan on the long-term in a much more credible way (which is useful when looking for loans or private sponsorship).

Third, you have to focus both on the acquisition and retention of donors. Both have a cost, but a different cost behavior. Indeed, for acquisition, the marginal cost of each donation decreases overtime; retention however has a return after a certain point; regular donations become pure profit after having amortized all the fixed acquisition costs and variable retention costs. A successful nonprofit optimizes both and formulates goals in terms of "donation mix" (the ratio of first-time donors to regular donors/total donors is a useful metric).

DONORS' ACQUISITION

You might be wondering why donors' asset is so valuable? Well first it is because getting people to send you money is not automatic. It is not just about sending an email with a link to your website, hoping that they will make a donation. Moreover, organic growth of your organization is not an accurate predictor of your donors' base growth. You have to demonstrate like we have seen earlier, that you can provide value and that you are trustworthy.

Plus, there is a natural erosion of your donors' base due to a wide range of factors over which you do not have control. Some people stop giving because they no longer can afford it, others because they have other priorities, some finally because their initial expectations have not been fulfilled. Maybe a yearly diagnostic of this attrition based on data analysis and donors' feedback could help you better identify the drivers of friction in order to mitigate them, but if you are not experiencing dramatic erosion, the costs of such analysis could be too high for what it is worth.

The question would be then; how to organically grow the number of donors? You have to understand it as a function of your exposure and of the perceived value of your organization.

First, you have to increase your exposure in a number of ways. Organizing events that favor proximity and human contact is a good start, as it allows to create interpersonal relationships between the members, fostering a common identity and networking. Word of mouth will be stronger as members will talk to non-members they know about their social involvement. Being active in the community is also useful, as you demonstrate to the broader public that your organization exists and lives up to its ambition to bring change. It will improve your local base and will help you maintain a grassroots movement that is anchored in communities.

Third, you will have to target visible and important causes that are relevant to the public. While it may sound opportunistic, do not forget that donors are ultimately people who think like you that the cause you are defending is worth fighting for, but do not have the time or energy to do so. You need to think of your cause as a "market," with a number of "customers" (your donors) and ambition to target the maximum amount of people willing to help. Moreover, you can contribute to improvements in local areas by segmenting your goals and acting on a small scale.

Do not hesitate to tackle issues and mobilize local communities around problems the government or other actors cannot solve or do not have the incentives to. It will be a convincing demonstration of the value you can provide society with, as well as an opportunity to show people how your organization works and who are the people behind the brand. Finally, it is crucial to leverage the power of the internet to enhance visibility, promote your activities and communicate around your values and agenda. We will talk about this aspect in Chapter 6.

You also have to work on your perceived value. The members you accept into your organization are your brand ambassadors, they represent your values and your ideals wherever they go, live and work. Therefore, they are the most reliable tellers of your trustworthiness and integrity. Do not be afraid of being selective when recruiting members, as an organization is not about numbers but quality and effectiveness. A hundred dedicated, serious and trustworthy members are worth more than thousands of inactive, unreliable ones.

Working on building your organizational culture is a key element, and it can be achieved through organizing team building events. Your media policy must also be carefully crafted, as you do not want to attract bad press or be associate with doubtful news organizations. The media relays of your nonprofit activities must all fit in a sensible communication and media strategy.

Finally and most importantly, you will have to appear as an active organization that is relevant in the landscape. You cannot isolate yourself in your own bubble out of purity or fear of compromise. It does not mean however that you will discard your values and integrity. But do not oppose concrete actions and interaction with other organizations with integrity. Be proactively looking for partnerships and opportunities to improve for example governmental and corporate practices surrounding the issue you are defending or promoting.

A WORD ON SPONSORSHIP

You have a lot of incentives to look out for corporate sponsorship, as it can be a game-changer. First, it can help you generate income that can contribute directly to taking your activities to another level of relevance, effectiveness and visibility. Second, it gives an opportunity for your employees, members and board members to network with corporate actors, therefore enabling them to broaden their expertise, their understanding of the scope of the mission and their particular skillsets. Moreover, it allows your nonprofit to tangibly integrate a network of active organizations, which will positively impact your reputation and your brand recognition. Corporate sponsorship is especially exciting since it is not charity; it is a project that both parties can expect to benefit from. It is a win-win proposal and if done well, can generate excellent value over time.

But why would a corporate sponsor you? Well it is simple because it ultimately would benefit from it. Indeed, it can be because as a specialized, focused nonprofit which has pooled dedicated talents around addressing a specific issue, you can act better than them. It can also be because their core activities are generating negative externalities your organization has a proven expertise in managing. Finally, it can be because they genuinely believe in improving life in the community you are both operating in, either as a way to satisfy their customers better or to respect regulations. So do not fool yourself, corporations sponsor nonprofits essentially out of self-interest. But both of you can benefit from this to increase your exposure, demonstrate your legitimacy in tackling issues and solving them across the board and enhance brand recognition as a result.

What forms can corporate sponsorship take? It can come as a large one-time donation, to fund a specific project on the short or medium run or it can be a long-term partnership, where both of you pool resources and expertise to tackle an issue on the long-term. Corporations have expectations in terms of the return on their investment. It can either be part of their marketing efforts to foster brand recognition or an element of their Corporate Social Responsibility policy. It can also help them enhance employees' satisfaction or customer perception of the values said corporations promote and acts on.

For you, it is about the money and the opportunity to work on a cross-organization project that will have to be serious enough to prompt support. It is a chance for your nonprofit to demonstrate that it is capable of working with serious people no matter their inner motivation, as long as it contributes to the cause you are defending. An organization that can put aside ideals and escapes the "purity syndrome" that can isolate nonprofits from the rest of society shows that it is genuinely motivated to achieve its goals. Finally, corporate sponsorship can also take the form of in-kind donations. The organization does not provide the nonprofit with cash but rather with goods, services or employees which can all contribute to advance the cause. While they are not bankable, in-kind donations are useful as they allow for better connection and networking opportunities for your staff and your organization.

HOW TO FIND A CORPORATE SPONSOR?

Now that you are convinced that corporate sponsorship can positively contribute to your organization's work, how can you find the right corporate sponsor?

First, you have to determine with exactitude what are your values, principles and mission. What are you fighting for and what is the approach you chose? What are your priorities, and what makes you stand out in the field of nonprofits that address the same issue as you do? Then, you need to do your research and scan for-profit organizations that share interests with you, that could benefit materially (in terms of pure economic profit, either directly or indirectly) from your success. The adequate corporate sponsor is the one that, while helping you, is ultimately helping itself. For example, by associating their brand to your organization, a for-profit can drive customer acquisition or retention, reinforce its perception as a virtuous actor or promote its products as a way of helping do good (since it generates money that funds a nonprofit). Therefore, prioritize those sharing the same demographics as yours, targeting a market where your organization has some recognition and vice versa.

This step is crucial as you do not want to associate your nonprofit with a corporation that does not share your values, your priorities, your target demographics or your way of seeing and doing things. An opportunistic mismatch can damage your reputation and credibility beyond repair and will not go well with members, volunteers and donors who thought they were supporting a genuine organization.

Finally, you will need to deploy a research team that will constantly keep an eye on market trends and corporate stories. Your organization will keep in touch with reality and spot interesting evolutions on which it could capitalize. For example it can help you notice that a corporation, after a scandal, has some public relations issues and is looking for a way to rebrand itself as a more responsible actor.

HOW TO PITCH FOR IT?
Once you have found a potential partner, how can you convince them that their organization can benefit from a partnership with you? For that you need to master the art of pitching, which is about proposing a detailed plan of action, which articulates both strategic vision and operational details. But it is mainly about showing where the value resides, for the company, your organization and the broader community.

You also need to ask yourself these questions. What are the drivers of your success? How many people can you expose to their brand in case they accept to sponsor you? How the association to your brand benefits them? How is working with you providing actual value? How can they reap a good return on investment by sponsoring you? It is about seeing things from their perspective rather than yours!

The initial contact is usually a cold call or mail, where you present your organization, stating your cause, the values you promote, the board members, the past achievements, the current projects and the near future. It is also essential to specify what is really unique about your organization and the way it does things. In the cold mail, present the project on which you could collaborate and why you chose specifically the corporation you are pitching to. It means that you need to detail how their values and ways of working fit with your organization's, how they can help you in succeeding in that endeavor and how they can benefit from such a collaboration.

If the initial contact proves to be fruitful, you will have to follow up with a pitch deck. It is usually a deck of PowerPoint slides where you present precise data in the form of due diligence. Due diligence is about the project and provides details about the process, methods and resources (including human resources) involved. You will have to present numbers, perspectives and actionable plans to achieve objectives that allow you to reach your end goal. In the pitch deck, emphasize on the alignment of interests, as the corporation's interests ultimately guide your actions.

It is because if you align your interests with theirs, they will be responsive and willing to consider the partnership. Note that producing an alignment of interests is not purely artificial; the initial scanning will allow you to identify the organization that has the most in common with you. Therefore, it is more about formatting than creating a false or exaggerated narrative.

If the pitch deck has proved to be compelling, the corporation will certainly schedule a meeting to formulate a partnership proposal that will detail the modalities of your collaboration, the nature and amount of the sponsorship.

THE ECONOMICS OF A NONPROFIT ORGANIZATION

In this section we will explore the accounting and economics of a nonprofit. You must understand these if you want to operate your nonprofit like a boss. Nothing can be left to randomness or chance.

Even though nonprofit organizations are not driven by the imperative of generating profits and redistributing it to "shareholders", they still have to be managed in a fiscally and economically responsible way. We must first consider that, because of the non-distribution clause, the sources of funds for a nonprofit equals the uses of funds. The generated net income is not redistributed in the form of dividends at the end of a fiscal year. It is fully invested in the organization's budget for its activities. There is, therefore, no way founders or managers can derive economic value out of a nonprofit. They only receive wages according to their responsibilities and the ratio between wages and overall budget is strictly monitored by the authorities so that no redistribution may occur through the allocation of excessively high wages. In this section we will detail the sources and uses of funds a nonprofit organization typically operates on.

SOURCES OF FUNDS: WHERE DOES THE MONEY COME FROM?

Nonprofit organizations generate the funds needed to run their activities in several ways. They mainly rely on donations. They can either be individual cash donations supporters and volunteers give because they believe in the nonprofit's mission and think that this particular organization can contribute positively. They can also be contributions from institutions and the government, with the rationale that private, specialized organizations can be more effective in tackling a specific issue than the government. Membership dues are also a key source of income for nonprofits; they rely heavily on their membership base to fuel money into the organization and contribute to the funding of activities they will take part in.

Fundraising takes two different forms: nonprofits can maintain continuous crowdfunding platforms to pool in individual donations (common with the rise of the Internet); it is a somewhat regular cash flow the organization needs to predict and optimize to have a strategic depth. Fundraising campaigns are punctual events, where the nonprofit gathers large-ticket donors are typically representing institutions to pool in cash and donations. These events are costly, so a nonprofit must analyze the return on investment of such events accurately. They can bring in a lot of money and shed light on an organization's work and initiatives; they remain however punctual and cannot be considered to be regular sources of funding.

Proceeds from the sale of merchandising can also constitute a large source of funds for a nonprofit. However, not all organizations can make merchandizing fit in their messaging and their income generation strategy, as it is particularly adapted to organizations which supply goods. Investment returns are also a non-core source of income for nonprofits. They invest a part of their resources in revenue-generating assets (like stocks or bonds, or delegate the management of their capital to financial institutions), which provides stable, somewhat predictable cashflows and returns over time.

Nonprofit organizations can also borrow money from financial institutions if they can demonstrate to have sufficient cash flow to support the leverage. The fall in interest rates the Western World has been experiencing for the last decade has opened up this niche credit market for banks. It allows them to have a positive impact on society and see it as a corporate social responsibility issue. On the other hand, it has made funding for nonprofits more accessible.

Corporate sponsorship can also contribute to funding a nonprofit's activity. While the organization must be careful in choosing corporate sponsors as its brand could be associated with eventual corporate malpractices, ultimately damaging its credibility as a genuine nonprofit, there are benefits in seeking corporate sponsorship. The rationale behind it is that firms are willing to sponsor nonprofits as they address the negative externalities their core activity generates. Like government sponsorship, corporate sponsorship assumes that a nonprofit would be more effective in dealing with specific problems than the firm itself. In a logic of optimizing capital use, sponsorship appears to be the best way. Moreover, it provides the firm with the opportunity to enhance its public image by appealing to consumers and economic operators who value the mission a sponsored nonprofit pursues.

USES OF FUNDS: WHERE DOES THE MONEY GO TO?
Nonprofit organizations use their funds to finance the administrative machine behind the organization. One of the main items on a nonprofit's budget is the wages it pays its employees. We must point out here that one of the measures of a nonprofit's performance and trustworthiness is the ratio between its overhead administrative costs and its total costs. If a nonprofit dedicates a disproportionate amount of its resources to wages, it means that the organization is not efficient enough and absorbs funds that should serve the mission directly.

Moreover, it could also indicate that founders and managers are funneling resources to themselves under cover of paid work. Donors are especially sensitive to this indicator as it is a summary measure of how much of their donation will go directly to the intended beneficiaries of the nonprofit's initiatives. However, insufficient funding for overhead administrative costs might damage the nonprofit's activities; hence managers

must find a balance, prompting them to optimize to the maximal level the administrative work. This is one of the drivers of stressful working conditions in the nonprofit sector that we will address in the human resources chapter.

Funds are also used to finance the nonprofit's core activity. This item depends on the nature of the activity; if a nonprofit provides goods and services, this item constitutes the main expenditure; if it is an advocacy group or a nonprofit that has an educational or religious vocation, it weighs less heavily on the organization's finances.

Resources must also be channeled to support volunteers, organize fundraisings and events. Marketing and communication is crucial to a nonprofit, however the impact of a campaign does not necessarily depend on the budget, as money only buys eye-balls when a nonprofit needs to establish deeper connections with viewers. This is why part of the communication budget will go to external consultants who will help the nonprofit calibrate their messages, target the right audiences, optimize their resources and craft impactful communication material.

A Short message from the Author:

Hey, are you enjoying the book? I'd love to hear your thoughts!

Customer Reviews

☆☆☆☆☆ 5
5.0 out of 5 stars ▾

5 star		100%	Share your thoughts with other customers
4 star		0%	
3 star		0%	Write a customer review
2 star		0%	
1 star		0%	

See all 5 customer reviews ›

Many readers do not know how hard reviews are to come by, and how much they help an author.

I would be incredibly thankful if you could take just 60 seconds to write a brief review on Amazon, even if it's just a few sentences!

>> Click here to leave a quick review

Thank you for taking the time to share your thoughts! Your review will genuinely make a difference for me and help gain exposure for my work.

STEP 4

BUILDING A MEMBERSHIP BASE AND BRAND RECOGNITION

A nonprofit organization that does not mobilize a membership base does not exist. It cannot have an impact in civil society since it is isolated from the rest and would not have the means (both human and financial) to organize events to draw attention to the cause it is promoting. A winning nonprofit is an organization that inspires, mobilizes and drives the people it attracts to its cause.

Members are the main asset of a nonprofit. Not only do they perform tasks that make the activity of a nonprofit possible, by helping in organizing events, intervening in public events, communicate around your brand and fundraise for you; the base is also an income-generating asset. As we have seen in the previous chapter, members do pay an annual membership fee, which flows constitute one of the rare stable sources of income for a nonprofit. It is therefore, vital for a starting nonprofit to capitalize on building its membership base.

Members sign up to become part of a nonprofit in exchange for an annual fee. Their involvement is up for renewal every year, which means that managers must have to take into consideration the aspirations of the member base to avoid high turnover rates. Such rates would negatively impact the work of a nonprofit, since it would reduce the pool of potential members and spread bad word of mouth, especially for grass-root organizations. There is a cost for acquiring members. It typically increases exponentially as the most accessible potential members need the least targeting. If a nonprofit does not increase its national network, it will reach a ceiling where attracting new members will eventually be impossible (the "market" for highly-motivated people towards a certain cause is generally small). Expanding your membership base does entail that you expand your footprint. There is also a cost for retaining members. As an organization, you will have to invest in team-building activities, quality events and administration to be able to create a positive experience for all parties involved. It is interesting to note that the higher the number of members gets, the lower the cost of retaining an individual member becomes.

The importance of members goes beyond economic considerations. Indeed, a strong feeling of belonging will make the work and activities of the organization much more efficient, as the stakeholders will identify with each other and the cause more strongly. Moreover, deploying a large membership base serves a bargaining chip when dealing with fundraising, borrowing or sponsorship.

To analyze the drivers of membership building, we must first ask the question: why would anyone join a nonprofit as a contributing member?

Members cite a wide range of reasons that prompt them to get actively involved in a nonprofit organization they believe in. They often want to have a positive impact helping the advancement of a cause that is dear to them; doing it in a structured way (membership, annual contribution, take part in the meetings etc.) is important. Second, members are somewhat insiders to the organizations they decide to join; it allows them to evaluate somewhat the level of efficiency, transparency and trustworthiness of a nonprofit. It can be seen as some kind of investigative work conducted by highly engaged citizens. Finally, some benefits are linked to member status, even though they are not automatic.

It is therefore clear then that the first step for building a strong membership base is to formulate a powerful message, articulated around a compelling communication and an impactful messaging. The cause, mission or issue your organization ambitions to embrace must be well-defined, and the means you will deploy to address it must be clarified and well-documented. Second, your nonprofit must demonstrate from the start that it runs on a culture that promotes solidarity, transparency, trustworthiness and accountability. Third, the managerial structure must be somewhat flat and inclusive, to leverage the membership you will acquire and to foster a participatory culture in the organization. While a charismatic founder will certainly contribute to attracting members thanks to his/her charisma and aura, checks and balances must be designed to ensure that the founder's syndrome does not go out of hand and antagonizes members.

HOW CAN YOU, THEREFORE, ATTRACT MEMBERS AND KEEP THEM IN THE ORGANIZATION?
You first need to define a well-designed membership program. It starts with

identifying the role members can play in the big picture of your organization: where do they fit? By isolating the purpose they can serve and the value they can bring, it is easy to target communication and branding on those aspects to maximize the effectiveness of your reach. Your membership program

must also feature a grid of fees and benefits that go along with said fees: members should be incentivized to subscribe to the plan that suits them best. You should not aim for fee maximization: it is better to have 1000 members who pay 10$ on average a year than 200 who contribute with 30$.

You have to design a signing-up system that is easy to understand, accessible and trustworthy. Use the right platform for you (we will cover the technological aspect in chapter 6) and ask for the minimum of information you need to organize your membership base effectively. A lengthy process is not advised, each minute that the potential member spends on the page filling up information can add to his/her frustration or impatience, prompting the potential member to abandon or get distracted.

After having crafted your membership program, you will have to get the word out. You need first to understand your target audience and talk to it. Draft some potential members' profiles, with their interests, their personal

beliefs and values as criteria and segments. Analyzing your target demographics is important as it will allow you to optimize your marketing efforts and reinforce your authenticity. Indeed, a passionate nonprofit will not target everyone in the hope of getting some attention, but will focus on those who seem to be eager to join and act. It is also important to leverage your organic networks by relying on employees, volunteers and board members to spread the word and list potential members in their inner circles.

You can gain your first members by "up-selling" volunteers into joining the program, with the benefits that go with it. Finally, invest in automation and digital marketing tools as they will help you minimize the amount of time spent and will make the best out of the raw data you derived from your targeting and segmentation. Putting forward the value you are offering to potential members should be your central point. A sign-up newsletter must also include a link to the sign-up page, to maximize conversion.

For nonprofits, it is useful to think of members as they were customers.

Indeed, they are the closest thing to customers since they are buying into your idea and project. They must be convinced that their initial investment in time, energy and money is worth it; plus, it is in your interest to have the highest renewal rate possible. It is crucial to distinguish in your membership base between first-time members and others, as this particular group has the highest turnover rate since they do not usually have the time to develop strong links that would convince them to stay. They are also the ones who reevaluate the most of their initial "purchase" decision. You must design a calibrated acquisition and retention strategy for them.

Finally, you need to create a true sense of community. Members must feel like belonging to an extended family, this is why you need to create bridges between individuals by setting up group chats for example. Organizing members-only events will also be decisive as it will allow for a real connection between members who have a lot in common. Plus, by developing personal relationships with others, members will have fewer incentives to leave. Their personal lives become increasingly associated with other members. You must also maintain regular communication with them, sending them weekly newsletters that inform them of the schedule, the initiatives, the opportunities, the challenges etc. Communication is key to maintain your membership base, but do not be tempted to spam them.

CONSIDERATIONS ABOUT YOUR BRAND
We typically do not associate the concept of the brand with nonprofits, as it sounds like something for-profit organizations develop to stand out in the crowded marketplace. But a brand is not only a trademark, but it is also a powerful summary of your values, your mission, your style and what sets you apart from those who are doing the same job as you. From this perspective, it is fundamental for a nonprofit to craft its brand image and we will see in this section how branding for nonprofits differs from for-profit branding.

There are some similarities between the two worlds as brands that serve the same purposes. Developing a strong brand allows an organization to stand out in a crowded market. Since nonprofits also operate on markets (if we consider members, donors and volunteers as "customers" who buy into your nonprofit's credibility), it is an essential feature. One of the challenges nonprofits face in their early steps is breaking the glass ceiling and establishing both the value they can provide the community with and how they differ from other nonprofits that address the same issues as they do. A good brand positioning can definitely help with that.

The conventional approach to branding in the nonprofit sector has often placed the brand at the center of the fundraising process. While it can be a powerful tool for that as it allows for the diffusion of branded merchandising that directly contributes to income generation, it somewhat limits the extent to which a brand can be useful. The dominant approach to branding focused on building visibility to maximize fundraising, it did not take into account the opportunities a good brand could provide a nonprofit with at the strategic level.

The development of an identifiable brand in the nonprofit world is generally seen as an essential step in an organization's growth. It constitutes an inflection point that is crucial to pass and manage in order to obtain nation-wide relevance and pursue the cause outside of an organization's native territory. Branding can help from a strategic perspective, as it allows to fix an identity and project short and long-term goals in terms of communication, membership building and internal cohesion. Moreover, it gives an organization more bargaining power and credibility when it comes to negotiating sponsorships, grants or partnerships. Nonprofits must therefore think about their brand like any other organization does: it is an intangible asset that has both an income-generating role and a managerial/marketing role.

There is a shift in brand management in large nonprofit organizations, as the emphasis has moved away from

income generation to strengthening social cohesion, identity and global impact. This is where branding in the nonprofit world differs from for-profit companies. Indeed, brands can be "shared," allowing larger organizations to sponsor other less-known initiatives that are in line with the mission or purpose they are promoting. Moreover, strong branding contributes directly to increased operational efficiency as it mechanically enhances the two drivers of performance in the nonprofit world: perceived value and intrinsic motivation. An omnipresent brand across the globe motivates employees, members, and volunteers much more than an obscure one, as it gives them at least the impression that their work is impactful indeed. Nonprofits have turned around the concept of branding to make it an internal governance tool and an essential part of the culture they are promoting.

But what exactly is a brand? It seems that it has a somewhat vague definition because it is not only the sum of a name, a slogan, a logo and a set of self-declared values and principles. Somehow when it comes to branding, the total is bigger than the sum of the individual parts. While a powerful brand does have all of the above items curated and well-designed, it also has something else. It is a psychological construct that is associated with an emotion. If in the for-profit world, a brand is seen as an experience the customer will remember and associates with positive emotional feedback; in the nonprofit world, a brand is a summary of the "what, why, how" that characterize the nonprofit.

STEP 5

HUMAN RESOURCES MANAGEMENT IN NONPROFIT ORGANIZATIONS

In this section, we will detail the managerial dynamics that characterize nonprofits. Again, to be able to manage your nonprofit like a boss, you first will have to understand who and what to manage, and in which ways.

We first need to determine the composition of the human resources in the nonprofit world. There are different types of workers who contribute either directly

or indirectly to the nonprofit activities. We can distinguish employees from volunteers and external consultants/advisors. Employees are conventional workers who enter a legally binding contract with a specific job description and outline of responsibilities. The nonprofit is their employer, which means that their interaction takes place in the framework of labor law. Employees are rewarded, albeit at lower rates than in the private sector. They often take responsibility for campaign organization, strategic planning, accounting/finance, human resources management and legal work.

Volunteers on the other hand have no contractual obligations towards the nonprofit. They are often the little hands that make a nonprofit impactful on the terrain. They contribute during events, meetings or demonstrations and have joined the nonprofit out of conviction for the purpose or mission the organization promotes. Volunteers constitute the operating base of any nonprofit, and since they are only attracted to volunteerism by conviction, managers and communication professionals must cater to their needs and always work on the perceived value of their organization and its work.

Finally, external consultants and advisors are independent contractors a nonprofit can recruit for a specific duration and mission to help solve a specific technical problem. They are not expected to feel engaged in the nonprofit's mission; they are hired to bring technical expertise the nonprofit might lack. For example, a nonprofit can hire IT consultants to improve the performance of its website or digital marketing consultants to develop a new marketing campaign that would leverage the power of social media.

Since employees do receive lower compensation for their skills than in the private sector, they need to demonstrate high intrinsic motivation for the cause and the work they will be performing. Human resources managers must therefore provide incentives, value and a positive experience to retain talents and decrease turnover rates. This can be done by focusing on delivering value that

contributes directly to achieving the organization's purpose, empowering employees and give them a role in the decision-making process. Hence nonprofits are much more reliant on periodic meetings where the hierarchical structure is flattened out and where employees can contribute to strategic planning and operational direction.

Volunteers on the other hand can bring generic or specialized skills to the organization, in a core or peripheral role and for variable engagement periods. They must be incentivized in the same manner employees are, even though volunteers have fewer responsibilities than employees. However, they must be associated to some degree to decision-making as they are expected to execute and act out the decisions. The engagement of volunteers is highly dependent on their motivation; therefore, it must be preserved by the nonprofit's actions overtime and managerial decisions must take into account the impact on brand and credibility.

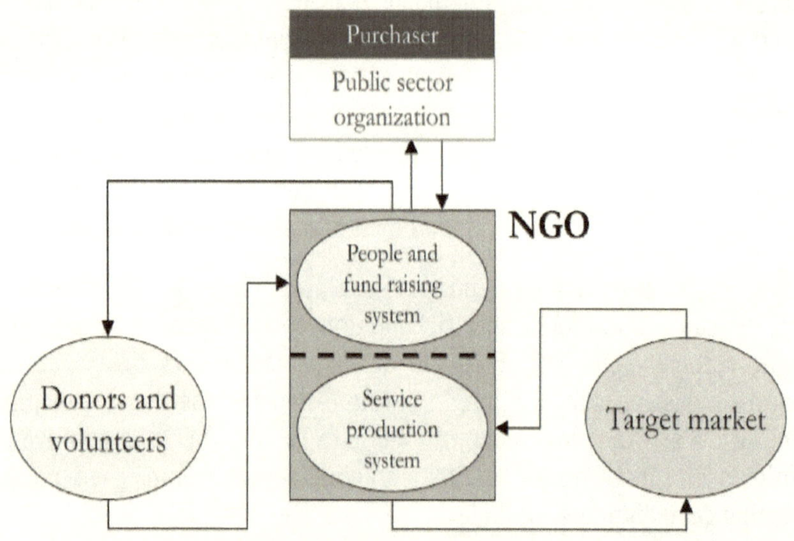

Multiple stakeholders, multiple accountabilities for nonprofit organizations. This is a "double market" situation, where the organization must cater to two different markets with misaligned interests and incentives.

THE CENTRALITY OF FOUNDING FIGURES

There is a specific problem in relation to nonprofit organizations. Since they often rely on emotional engagement with the public and potential members and volunteers, the founding figures who power a nonprofit during the initial stages often have high levels of charisma. Such psychological profiles tend to associate

the structure with their image. It, therefore, makes it hard for the nonprofit to evolve over time and leave some decision-making powers to non-founding figures who might be more competent or more aware of the current challenges that come with the mission. This centrality impacts the ability of founders to delegate work to others, to associate their organization to themselves (and vice versa) and to plan adequately for succession and transfer of responsibilities. There is a tendency for founding figures who find resonance in public to overtime cause governance problems in setting priorities, new objectives and goals or a strategic plan. They may also foster a culture that does not match the aspirations or the management model the nonprofit has to adopt to fulfill its purpose.

In the corporate world, the presence of shareholders balances out the centrality of founding figures. There are many examples where charismatic founders have been kicked out of the companies, they founded themselves and often managed with great success. We can consider the case of Travis Kalanick, founder and CEO of Uber until he had been forced to resign by the board of directors and activist shareholders, who blamed him for a toxic corporate culture and lack of transparency. Even though Kalanick was (and still is) one of the most influential entrepreneurs in Silicon Valley (and that he founded a company that is now worth $100 billion), the for-profit power structure allows for change at the head and the transfer of responsibility went on smoothly. Indeed, after Kalanick's resignation, Uber successfully filed for an Initial Public Offering (IPO) on the New York Stock Exchange, and ranked as the bigger in terms of emissions of shares in 2019.

Giving too much importance to founders has a price in the nonprofit world. According to Stephen Block and Steven Rosenberg, authors of a report quantifying founder's syndrome in 2002, founder-led organizations have smaller budgets, lack proper governance mechanisms to ensure balance of power and that they lack maneuverability in the face of paradigm shifts.

WAGE POLICY

We have seen that employees are usually expected to derive fewer incentives from their pay and more from their mission. However, it does not mean they are not entitled to a living wage. Labor laws apply to the nonprofit world, therefore imposing minimum wage and the legal number of working hours. Wage policy must take into account these limitations, but cannot go overboard with compensation. Indeed, tax-exempt status depends on the ratio of overhead administrative costs (which include wages) to the total costs, to avoid a disguised transfer of donations and other funds to employees. Hence employees in nonprofits know that this constraint will mechanically limit their pay.

Bonuses are authorized by the nonprofit regulations; however, the tax authorities rigorously oversee them because they could constitute a violation of the non-distribution clause. The variable remunerations can be determined based on specific performance indicators that are related to the role of each employee. For example, an employee in charge of overseeing

fundraising could receive a bonus if his/her actions directly contributed to raising more money than it was expected. Note that variable compensation is part of the overall salary, not an additional item. Therefore it is also computed in the ration we have mentioned earlier.

Compensation for executives is a trickier subject. Good practice states that the board of directors must unanimously agree on executives' pay to ensure maximum independence, fairness and transparency. Pay does include other benefits like health insurance. It is understood that executives' pay must be somewhat competitive with respect to the private sector to attract talents and compensate responsibility and the duties of representation. However, it is still expected to be lower than in the private sector as executives have to demonstrate a motivation to work that goes beyond pure monetary compensation. To set a benchmark, the board of directors usually sets an independent body to examine the landscape and come up with a range. Negotiation ensues and the compensation package is approved both by the executive and the board of directors.

BOARD OF DIRECTORS

The board of directors is the central organ of a nonprofit. Board members have the responsibility of ensuring good governance principles by promoting transparency, accountability, fairness, inclusiveness, and efficiency. Managing a nonprofit legitimately and effectively implies these values because as we have seen in this book, it constitutes an essential criterion for getting and keeping the nonprofit status.

Board members have a wide range of responsibilities, the main one being appointing an executive director or CEO who will concretely steer the organization and work to advance the cause. The board has to evaluate the candidates and decide on which basis they should appoint an executive. They also have to discuss the executive's compensation and have the authority to monitor his/her activities and evaluate the effectiveness with which the executive works.

Individual board members also have the responsibility of representing the organization in other governance organisms they may participate in. Therefore, they have an obligation to be in phase with the values and principles the organization stands for. They play an essential role in fundraising as they are the public figures of a nonprofit and a guarantee that the organization is credible and trustworthy. Since they do not usually derive any compensation from their role on the board of directors, the members are expected to be impartial, non-interested stakeholders. It puts them in the best position to arbitrate conflicts of interest between other stakeholders in an organization. This is why their core values and principles are so important; they represent a guarantee that they will uphold their mission.

Networks and eco-systems come in handy when picking board members. Since they are not usually eligible for compensation, they often have a main professional engagement that goes beyond your organization. By networking and building bridges in the community you are operating in, you can come across ethical, loyal and fair individuals who have the skills and experience to monitor your nonprofit's overall performance and its employees.

Finally, the board of directors is not a sacred institution and has to be brought together by fostering a culture of good governance, fairness and competence. Do not hesitate to organize cross-organization formative sessions to get your board members to meet other actors or to learn from past experiences.

MISALIGNMENT OF INTERESTS AND INCENTIVES

Nonprofits are often characterized by resource mismanagement and poor planning. It is mainly since there are poor checks and balances on the work of employees, as they are not motivated by economic gain. It poses a question of performance management in an era where it is mainly driven by quantitative indexes pertaining to efficiency and effectiveness. For example, an employee can formulate a new program within an organization without properly conducting due diligence and thus misestimating liabilities and costs. Since there are no shareholders to hold employees and managers accountable because of investor oversight, it often happens that these programs, which are poorly thought out, end up putting nonprofits in objective difficulties.

Moreover, there is a competence problem in nonprofits. Indeed, nowadays, one of the most important drivers for professional involvement and performance is remuneration. A disproportionate share of new graduates is simply not attracted to working in a nonprofit, where wages are lower than in the private sector. At the same time, the increasing cost of a college education has put a financial strain on most of them. Nonprofits need to gather talents as they work on complex issues and have to act in innovative, out-of-box ways to promote their mission and values. Hiring has long been seen as a secondary priority for managers, and it has had a detrimental impact on the organizational efficiency of nonprofits. Worse, talents are increasingly looking up to nonprofits as millennials and generation Z are considered to be much more sensitive to public issues like climate change, income inequality and human rights. But they are for the most part siphoned by international organizations and well-known nonprofits, like the UN, Amnesty International or Doctors without Borders (MSF). This situation leaves independent, grass-root movements totally uncompetitive on the labor market as they cannot offer similar compensation and cannot promise candidates that they will have a bigger impact working with them than working with the United Nations.

Setting compelling incentives to nonprofit work is crucial because departing employees have cited, amongst other reasons for their departure, the ill-adapted level of compensation for an often strenuous, implacable work under stressful conditions and with often inadequate resources. Employees are simply giving too much for the cause, while they could be getting much more for the same amount of effort or less in the private sector and still have an impact on reality. Such human resources approach mechanically limits the pool of potential candidates as the nonprofit sector is not competitive for prospective workers in the face of private and government placements. Only mission-driven, highly compassionate individuals can realistically consider joining a nonprofit as a full-time employee.

There is a solution for nonprofits, though. When we examine the criteria, employees choose to evaluate a work opportunity and experience, a good working environment generally ranks higher than high salary or bonus packages. Nonprofits must aim in providing this kind of highly valued work experience, as they have the means to truly foster an organizational culture centered around this priority, to retain talents and create, in the long run, a benchmark for nonprofit work.

STEP 6

LEVERAGING TECHNOLOGY, NETWORKS AND ECO-SYSTEMS

HARNESSING THE POWER OF THE INTERNET
Real assessment of the reality of nonprofit work in the current era shows that nonprofits do not exploit to the full extent the Internet's potential. While nonprofits have been leveraging emailing and automated marketing, they still do not capitalize on the nearly infinite potential that the Internet presents them with.

We can identify three ways nonprofit organizations use the internet to project their agenda. First, they experiment with setting up a digital reputation and image

that will serve as a base for future investments. Second, they leverage the broadcast power of online communication, which has one of the best returns on investment for marketing and communication budgets. Moreover, the progress made in online advertising allows for scientific targeting of the audience, based on big data gathering and analysis. Third, the internet allows for interactive dialog, both in the organization (as we discussed earlier, internal communication towards members is crucial for retaining a solid base) and outside the organization (chatbots and live chat sessions to increase awareness, to create personal contact with potential members and to give a human face to the organization)

Nonprofits must also step up its web site design by going beyond the logic of an online brochure. Most of the nonprofits set up websites as a way of plainly informing visitors on the issue, the organization with an invitation to email them if they are looking to join. It is a purely passive approach to an online presence that does not engage at all with visitors. A website is no longer a catalog, it is an online experience that influences massively how your brand is perceived. Beyond the design, the interface and the content, the organization of the website itself allows to emphasize the priorities and to illustrate the actions and initiatives an organization has conducted. Moreover, with advanced marketing tools, a website becomes a hub for potential members and insiders to get in touch and interact with you.

SOCIAL MEDIA IS THE NEW INTERNET

Facebook's Mark Zuckerberg was right in envisioning his social media as more than a gateway to Internet, but as the Internet itself. In its aggressive growth campaign in developing countries, Facebook has sponsored internet access in exchange for its application is included as a basic feature in the data plans of new customers. For millions of internet users in the developing world, Facebook is effectively their Internet.

This is why nonprofits must focus on building a relevant social presence. It is increasingly important for them to have a scientific approach to digital marketing on social media by understanding the underlying algorithms and business models specific platforms run on. Indeed, for social media, algorithms state priorities and indicators that are, in some way or another, directly linked to profit-drivers for the company designing, hosting and managing the platform. Calibrating messaging, imagery, audiovisuals, and community management according to each platform's algorithms is, therefore, essential to derive the maximal value. For nonprofits, it is advised first to hire external consultants who can first determine the priorities and the means a specific organization can target and mobilize. Then, a mature organization should aim at building an in-house digital marketing and social media team to be able to have a flexible content creation team and community management that is adaptable to strategic orientations.

Content creation on social media is what propels an account. Messages should be curated from a design perspective, on target and explicit. They should be tailored for the specific audience an organization is aiming to reach. Big data must be leveraged to be able to adequately identify the users who are the most susceptible to your messaging; it will also indicate the levers on which you can act in order to derive maximal engagement and drive conversion. Finally, social media are not only platforms for content, and they allow every party to communicate with others, interacting around a specific post or a brand and leaving comments, reviews and recommendations.

WHERE CAN THE INTERNET HELP?

The internet can assist nonprofits in a variety of ways, beyond reach and membership acquisition. Indeed, it can help with publicity, education, fundraising, recruitment, service delivery, advocacy and research. Moreover, the benefits the internet provides can be enhanced thanks to the integration of local branches to the collective effort. While these uses do overlap with functions relevant to government agencies and for-profit organizations, internet use for nonprofits differs as it focuses on fundraising and advocacy rather than marketing or data gathering and analytics.

When it comes to fundraising, it is statistically obvious that there is no correlation between fundraising proceeds and internet presence. Being on the internet is not enough to leverage online presence for fundraising. While it has been mainly due to the reluctance of people to make first-time donations on the internet, it is especially because most nonprofits do not adopt the right communication strategies. An organization has first to lay the groundwork for building an online reputation on the criteria we have already discussed (accountability, trustworthiness, transparency, genuine engagement) to prompt first-time donors into donating. Therefore, a nonprofit should not aim for direct appeal for funds but rather demonstrate that it is worthy of receiving donations, because it will put them to good use.

Regarding recruitment, internet has proven to be much more effective. First, it is because recruiting volunteers is primarily driven by visibility, which the internet provides if the nonprofit actually deploy a communication strategy that focuses on reach, branding, and value display. Moreover, nonprofits have started to leverage the existence of job boards across the world to post openings for volunteer roles, branding them as "professional experiences" that can be valuable for students and young graduates. Online presence has also expanded the range of works that can be done by volunteers. Virtual volunteers are now a thing with the emergence of remote work; volunteers can work on web design, content writing etc.

Having an online presence also contributes to raising awareness surrounding the issues and causes you are fighting for. Non-profit organizations invest a lot of resources in educating the public and other stakeholders, producing a lot of materials to advance the cause. The Internet allows for cost reduction as videos, graphics and blogs are cheaper to generate and maintain, and can be distributed across the area of interest for practically no cost, compared to published material. Moreover, quality materials and adequate communication reinforce the perceived credibility of an organization; it does require however a somewhat substantial investment in human resources, as content must be curated, updated, and distributed.

HOW ORGANIZED NETWORKS OPERATE; WHERE DO MEMBERS DERIVE VALUE?
Networks that connect different actors across a specific geographical area are key to generate value overtime and drive collaboration across sectors. Members of a nonprofit are sensitive to the opportunities the organization they have joined can provide them with by connecting them to like-minded people.

A nonprofit can leverage the advantages of networking by striking collaborations with government agencies and for-profit corporations. Collaborating around specific issues with these partners does not mean that the organization will have to bear some reputational responsibility in case of malpractice; it means the nonprofit will strive to include relevant actors when planning actions or drafting strategy.

For example, an organization that advocates for environmental protection will certainly benefit from creating bridges with environmental agencies and companies which are looking for commercially viable ways to tackle the issue.

Members derive value from such initiatives since they have the opportunity to be exposed to real-world problems in a context that goes beyond the organization. They can get first-hand accounts and perspectives from other actors involved in the cause they are defending. They can also benefit from shared experiences and see how different approaches can contribute to solving the issue. It also gives them a chance to personally network with other individuals, establishing contact with resources that could eventually be interested in collaborating again. Finally, members will have tangible evidence that the work they do is meaningful, that they provide value to the community and that your organization is truly committed to the mission.

DERIVING BENEFITS FROM ECO-SYSTEMS
The goal of strategic planning is to make the organization's capacities, its mission and values and its immediate environment all fit, in a somewhat harmonious alignment of interests and incentives to generate value across the

community. The recent trends have been focusing a lot on networking, building hubs and organizing activities in a multi-level, multi-channel way. It is indeed helpful for a starting nonprofit as it will allow focusing on its core activities while benefiting from the expertise of other players in the networks. Rather than aiming at solving problems individually, nonprofits can leverage the technology and the increased connectivity to foster collaboration across sectors. Such initiatives can take the form of pro-active consulting with for-profit firms, bringing in additional income but also having a tangible impact on the real world by adjusting the behavior of for-profit actors to take into consideration the cause you are promoting. It is all about identifying the players who share your vision and who have the same drive as you for tackling an issue. You probably will not agree on the scope of tackling a specific issue. For example, if you are advocating for a cause nation or worldwide, you might have to collaborate with

an entity that just wants to solve that problem at its level. But small contributions that go in the sense of your mission not only contribute incrementally to changing the world, it also provides your staff with hands-on experience and makes your organization more credible.

The eco-system approach can yield benefits for all entities and institutions; from a commercial standpoint, the logic of ecosystems is best found in creating joint-ventures or in mergers & acquisitions. The nonprofit world can also leverage this approach by maximizing value sharing across the networks. It is, therefore, relevant as it allows a nonprofit to broaden its strategic impact on the community by advancing its ideals and its goals; since it is its main object, such an organization will benefit from it.

STEP 7

CAMPAIGNING

BASICS OF CAMPAIGNING: DIFFERENT APPROACHES, TOOLS, SCOPES AND GOALS
WHAT DOES CAMPAIGNING FOR A NONPROFIT IMPLY?

Campaigning is the most proactive way to draw support and attract eyeballs to your organization and to the cause you are promoting. It shares a lot with for-profit marketing campaigning, as it mobilizes the same toolbox and skillset. The differences lie though in the object that is put forward: for-profit organizations communicate about the value they provide customers with and the unique twist, features or design the product presents.

The starting point of a for-profit campaign is customer needs and desires and the product or service is presented as the most optimal answer to those needs and desires. Targeting is based on customer segments, which distinguishes customers in terms of purchasing power, purchase behavior, willingness to pay, needs and taste. Marketing professionals draw up accurate metrics to evaluate them, and they serve as key performance indicators (KPIs) to measure the effectiveness of a campaign.

However, for a nonprofit, the reference point around which a campaign revolves is the importance of the cause they are advocating for and how this particular organization can be trusted to be part of the solution. The organization itself is on the front page, it is the way it is doing things and the values it acts on that are presented to potential volunteers, donors and members. Targeting is based on values, ideas, expectations and willingness to engage, all of which are harder to quantify. It is therefore vital to have a true feeling and understanding of the drivers of engagement in the "markets" you act in.

For both fields creativity is the fuel of any successful marketing campaign. When it comes to marketing the main value-generating asset is the ability to craft a compelling message that succeeds in capturing the values and the spirit of a brand while perfectly delivering the point, without ambiguity or unnecessary talking. A common trend that comes up when studying the history of marketing is that, while the ability to buy media exposure is important, it is creative messaging as defined above that makes the difference between an impactful, effective campaign and steamroll advertising. It is important to gather resources of course to fund the acquisition of media channels but it is crucial to have the right people.

When gathering a team to design and leading the thinking for campaigns, you will have to take into consideration the skill set of course, but also the values, the mindset and the work ethic that power them. We

have seen how hard it can be for nonprofits to attract and retain talents in the face of more competitive compensation in the private sector; that is why values and a genuine will to contribute to the cause and spread the message are essential. Genuine motivation is what powers a campaign in the making.

DIFFERENT APPROACHES

We can distinguish a wide variety of ways and means to structure a nonprofit campaign. Choosing the right way of communicating with the individuals and groups you target depends essentially on the behavior you want to trigger. Are you looking to simply increase the public awareness around the issue you are tackling or attract donations?

If the primary goal of your campaign is advocacy, it will first have to convey a precise message that expresses your point, your stance of the issue, why it is important to act and why your nonprofit can do it. You need to inform the audience, it is mainly a pedagogical approach that aims at educating the public; however it can take many forms; from a cognitive approach that involves facts to an emotional campaign that intends on shocking the public and is appealing to emotions and feelings (the *logos* and the *pathos*). Moreover, advocacy campaigns focus on the invitation to dialog and communicate reciprocally, as it is usually performed by volunteers going to the contact in public places and on social media to create organic links between the nonprofit and the public.

Merchandising is a more customer-value driven approach, as it intends to market a product which is presented as an indirect way of donating, while in the same moment giving buyers something in return and an opportunity to display your brand. Recent trends in merchandising go beyond the simple items with a logo but demonstrate that a distinctive, aesthetic product is a more successful driver of adoption. While merchandising is not per se a campaigning technique, it can be added to an advocacy campaign as a fundraising driver and can generate mass adoption if it leverages both the power of social media and e-commerce. Nonprofits have started to promote a cause by offering sympathizers an opportunity to acquire limited miscellaneous objects that contribute to solving the issue. The case of the nonprofit 4ocean is a case study as the nonprofit aims at cleaning the oceans from plastic by recycling it to manufacture limited edition bracelets, which is sold to sympathizers and supporters as a direct way to contribute to the cause. Their well-crafted slogan states that buying one bracelet contributes directly to removing one pound of plastic.

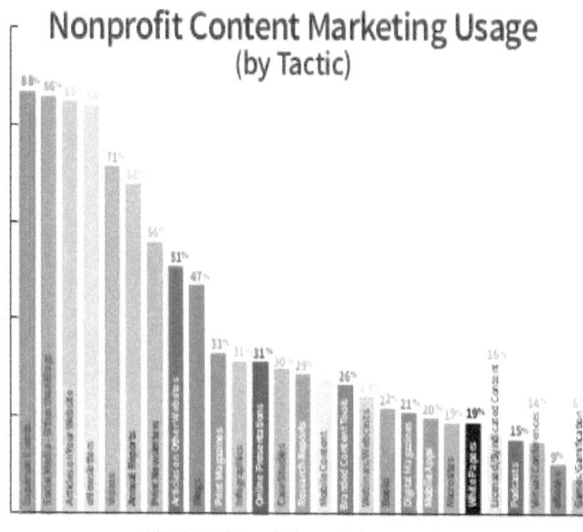

Leveraging the internet also allows for regular, curated and targeted communications with your target audience, as the power of email marketing is a key ingredient for advocacy campaigns. Indeed, newsletters that keep updated donors, members, volunteers and sympathizers and give them insights about the issues are effective for maintaining relationships overtime and increase both acquisition and retention rates. It is important not to make into fully dedicated to advertising but to adopt a newsletter policy that focuses mainly on information rather than promotion. Spamming is also a misuse of this tool and can have for obvious reasons negative returns over time.

Social media, in particular, have proven to be especially efficient in creating engagement that is strong enough to generate donations, in a way never seen before at this scale. Indeed, the last decade has seen spectacular success for many nonprofits as they exploited the trend of social media challenges. The concept allows users to not only share original content for a positive reason, but it also involves them personally and engages them as soon as they adhere to it. The ALS campaign for example has generated hundreds of millions of viral videos that have contributed to raising the visibility worldwide for virtually no cost. Such engagement translated in more than $115 million in donations, effectively demonstrating that viral content can serve as a powerful promotion if used by a serious organization that can prove itself trustworthy to users.

To better understand the way these different approaches and tools can be used in a coordinated way to maximize efficiency, we will take the example of the BatKid campaign. BatKid, in 2014, drew worldwide engagement as a San Francisco child's Make-a-Wish demand was filmed and shared across social platforms.

The most interesting thing about this campaign is how it has been able to identify and leverage its digital assets to produce the maximum result. The content agency that took in charge of the promotion of the situation accepted to do the work pro-bono and mobilize its network of thousands of small and mid-cap influencers to spread the

story and curate the content according to the different audiences. It implied a thorough analysis of the content strategy, the various targets the network could reach and how to preserve authenticity and spontaneity. Indeed we could consider on a marginal level that this campaign was also a way for the content agency to generate attention around its approach to marketing and its willingness to take on causes. But it also provided visibility to Make-a-Wish that saw a peak of 1000 visitors per second on its website, indirectly contributing to attracting new donors and participants to the foundation and its other less-known programs. Finally, it allowed for the organization of a significant event as 20,000 came to see the outcome of the campaign, creating genuine personal contact and empowering all stakeholders.

EXAMPLES OF SUCCESSFUL NONPROFIT CAMPAIGNS

A successful campaign often implies to get out of the comfort zone and constantly seek to renew the appeal. It is challenging for well-established organizations to do so

because of the increasing hierarchical pressure, which comes with scale. Decisions are taken by consensus on the leading figures' ideas and propositions, which stifles creativity and produces mediocre engagement material.

A good example of a big organization stepping out of its comfort zone to take a ground-breaking initiative could be the emoji campaign of the World Wide Fund (WWF). In 2015, the organization saw the potential of social media and providing a platform for user engagement. It launched an emoji campaign, designing 17 emoji representing endangered species. A user would donate 0.10€ for each tweet featuring WWF's emoji. It has prompted a wave of support, raking nearly 600,000 mentions in the first days of the campaign.

The lesson to be learned here is that you need to experiment, albeit with minimum risk and cost, to find the excellent recipe. WWF identified emoji as being a subject of interest for young users of social media, but it also understood its very nature: a channel of communication. It has also confirmed that the main

driver of engagement with nonprofit campaigns is inclusion. All successful social media campaigns have placed user engagement at the center of the process. It is empowering your audience to act both as donors and relays of your advocacy efforts is the key.

Another example can be found in the internet campaign launched by Love Has No Labels. This organization acts to tackle gender and sexual discrimination and had launched a campaign inviting users to take a questionnaire that helped them identify their individual biases. The organization did well not to stigmatize participants; better, it set a platform of dialogue and engagement with the users and between the users themselves. It also followed up by providing a trove of documentation, articles, and graphics that provide participants with a deeper understanding of the issues of gender and sexual discrimination. This has proven to be particularly effective because it not only provided value to participants (it is very hard to identify the biases we hold, especially when it comes to discrimination), it has also provided them with an opportunity to discuss and learn.

LESSONS TO BE LEARNED FROM FAILED CAMPAIGNS
The ALS campaign of 2014 had both been a resounding success for the organization and a proof of concept. By raising $115 million thanks to the viral Ice Bucket Challenge, ALS demonstrated that a social media campaign focused on user engagement rather than everyday advocacy provided insane returns on investment. It drew the participation of celebrities who gave the challenge worldwide visibility, hence bringing billions of users to hear the message and hundreds of millions to contribute to the cause. However, it proved to be a one-shot concept. Indeed, a couple of years later, ALS tried to replicate the same communication strategy, launching again an Ice Bucket Challenge strictly identical to the first one. It did not gather nearly as much attention as the first edition and proved to be a failure. It is mainly because ALS did not understand that internet trends

have a life cycle and cannot be imposed on users when they lose visibility and relevance. It is somewhat disappointing to see that what drew attention to the first campaign was more its ability to provide users with new modes of communication between themselves (challenging one another or feeling the social pressure of participating/giving). The core subject of the ALS campaign was only secondary in the minds of social media users. The lesson here would be not to overuse a good recipe. If a marketing strategy works exceptionally well at a certain point, do not insist on squeezing it out. Let it die gracefully and try to sustain the same spirit and concept rather than the form.

Another lesson can be derived from the 2009 ad campaign the Movember nonprofit launched. Movember is a nonprofit working on men's health issues, from mental health to male-specific diseases like prostate cancer. It became known when it organized its first Movember campaign, which men worldwide to grow mustaches during the entire month of November in a show of support for the cause. In 2009 it had released a video that showed a group of men beating to death a character dressed as a tumor. It backfired immediately because of the graphics and the explicit association between manhood and physical violence.

The ad campaign had been outsourced by the nonprofit to a traditional advertising firm, which itself is a mistake. While you can, of course, seek advice and counsel from professionals, do not rely entirely on them or you will risk losing your unique voice in the process. The second mistake was to air the commercial without any critical approach being considered. While the metaphor is itself harmless (help us beat –quite literally- cancer), the way it had been done was counterproductive and conveyed negative association in the minds of viewers.

CONCLUSION

We have listed in this book the seven main elements you need to study to build a solid base for your new nonprofit organization. This guide is both an introduction to nonprofit entrepreneurship and a compilation of advice and remarks to guide you during the demanding yet exciting startup phase.

We have underlined the importance of choosing the right legal framework for your activity and governance model. While this book does not pretend to be exhaustive when it comes to legal considerations, hopefully, it has been able to give you starting points and recommendations that will guide you.

We have clarified the economic aspect of running a nonprofit, underlying its functioning from a financial and accounting perspective. Nonprofits are ultimately businesses whose goal is to generate resources to tackle an issue rather than provide economic value to its investors. We can safely say that nonprofits are in the business of transparency, accountability, trustworthiness, ethics and public interest. This type of organization competes between themselves in those categories, as they are the most relevant indicators of their ability to tackle a public issue.

We have highlighted the managerial challenges inherent to the nonprofit model. Everything from recruitment to wage policy and governance is different, as monetary incentives for individuals are reduced to the bare minimum. The legal obligations nonprofits face make them unattractive professional opportunities for money-driven individuals, as the rationale behind the non-distributive clause severely constrains wage policy. Nonprofits are naturally less hierarchical and thrive on inclusion and inner motivation, but they suffer from founder syndrome. The centrality of founders can sometimes affect the flatness of the structure and favor the concentration of authority under the founder.

We have insisted on the importance of investing in technology and adopting the new communication practices the internet has consecrated. The predominance of social media is visible at so many levels. It allows for a more precise and scientific understanding of the market and of the targeted demographics, thanks to data analysis. It offers new and innovative communication channels that favor user engagement. It finally offers privileged access to the youth, the most present and active group online. It is crucial as younger generations are more willing than their parents to invest or get involved in nonprofits and are more sensitive to public issues.

Finally, we have provided a guide to campaigning for nonprofits, exposing the different approaches, tools, and scopes. By analyzing real-life cases, we have illustrated the theory with examples and showed the limits of some concepts when they are applied to specific situations. Finally, we have identified a series of mistakes and misconceptions that have impacted the effectiveness of past campaigns.

We hope this introduction to the fascinating and impactful world of nonprofits has helped you understand the full process and the main drivers of success and failure.

BIBLIOGRAPHY

For more insights about nonprofit organizations and the specific challenges that are associated to this world, here are some books you should read. Part of this e-book has been inspired by this list.

- **Braun, A.** : The Promise of a Pencil.
- **Novogratz, J.** : The Blue Sweater.
- **Sinek, S.** : Start with why: How great leaders inspire everyone to take action.
- **Leroux Miller, K.** : The nonprofit marketing guide.
- **Kanter, B; Fine, A.** : The networked nonprofit
- **Crutchfield, L; McLeod Grant H**. : Forces for Good, the six practices of high-impact nonprofits.
- **Garry, J.** : Joan Garry's guide to nonprofit leadership.

The end... almost!

* 9 7 9 8 7 2 8 8 6 3 1 3 7 *